# DAVID'S REDHAIRED DEATH

*Sherry Kramer*

**BROADWAY PLAY PUBLISHING INC**
New York
www.broadwayplaypublishing.com
info@broadwayplaypublishing.com

DAVID'S REDHAIRED DEATH
© Copyright 2012 by Sherry Kramer

First printing: June 2006
this edition, revised: August 2012
I S B N: 978-0-88145-313-3

Book design: Marie Donovan
Page make-up: Adobe Indesign
Typeface: Palatino
Printed and bound in the U S A

# ABOUT THE AUTHOR

Sherry Kramer is the recipient of an N E A, a
New York Foundation for the Arts Fellowship, a
McKnight National Fellowship, and a commission
from the Audrey Skirball-Kenis Theater Project. Her
plays have been produced in the United States and
abroad, and include productions at Actors Theater
of Louisville's Humana Festival, Yale Repertory
Theater, The Second Stage, Woolly Mammoth Theater,
Soho Repertory Theater, Ensemble Studio Theater,
Annex Theater, InterAct Theater, and the Theater
of the First Amendment. She was the first national
member of New Dramatists.  Plays include: WHEN
SOMETHING WONDERFUL ENDS; DAVID'S
REDHAIRED DEATH (The Jane Chambers Award);
THE WALL OF WATER (L A Women in Theater
Award); WHAT A MAN WEIGHS (Weissberger
Playwriting Award, New York Drama League Award,
The Marvin Taylor Playwriting Award); A THING
OF BEAUTY; HOW WATER BEHAVES; THE BAY
OF FUNDY: AN ADAPTATION OF ONE LINE
FROM THE MAYOR OF CASTERBRIDGE; THINGS
THAT BREAK; THE WORLD AT ABSOLUTE
ZERO; THE MAD MASTER; THE LONG ARMS OF
JUPITER (a croquet performance piece); PARTIAL
OBJECTS; THE LAW MAKES EVENING FALL;
THE MIDDLE OF THE DAY; A PERMANENT
SIGNAL; THE RULING PASSION; THE RELEASE

OF A LIVE PERFORMANCE; THE MASTER AND MARGARITA (a singing-theatre adaptation with composer Margaret Pine); NANO AND NICKI IN BOCA RATON; NAPOLEON'S CHINA (a play with music, with Ann Haskell and Rebecca Newton); ABOUT SPONTANEOUS COMBUSTION; IVANHOE, ARK.; and THE RULING PASSION. She holds M F As from the Iowa Writers' Workshop (Fiction) and the Iowa Playwrights Workshop, and teaches playwriting at Bennington College, and regularly at The Michener Center for Writers at the University of Texas, Austin, and the Iowa Playwrights' Workshop, where she was previously head of the workshop.

# CHARACTERS

JEAN, *her hair is deep, rich, dark auburn red. She is thirty.*

MARILYN, *her hair is bright red, true, light red. She is thirty.*

TWO STAGE TECHNICIANS, *tall, darkhaired men. The stage technicians are play enablers—they transform the ordinary world into the redhaired world within our sight, they become McDonald's employees on demand, they ready Jean for her journey—they do whatever is needed. They belong to the play, not to themselves, they are part of the play's system of death.*

*The first New York production had ten Technicians—all young, tall, darkhaired men wearing dark suits, as if dressed for a funeral—they enabled the play, and gave extra signal to the base line system of death. Technician number is up to each production, but two is the optimal minimum.*

# SETTING

*The redhaired world is created, and then lost during the play—a transforming, non-static setting, constantly evolving or de-evolving.*

*The Redhead's bed is the center focus of the play. But her bed is not an ordinary one—elements of the natural world encroach on the man-made aspects of everything associated with her. The bed may be outside, nestled in a woodland glen surrounded by trees even before the transformation begins. The 1985 Royal Blue Pontiac Tempest should be suggested in some way, and all set pieces should have active interaction with the characters and the two stage technicians.*

*All sound effects are created by the technicians, including music—a redhaired-world melody, on vibes or some other bell toned instrument is recommended, as is scoring throughout the play.*

*Costumers note: Redheads have been known to wear deep forest green. They don't always wear pink or red.*

# ACT ONE

JEAN: *(To the audience)* There was a time a person had
only a hundred deaths, at best. In remote, isolated
places forty or fifty had to do. When a man died, the
only people who had his death were the members
of his family, and those close enough to know him,
day by day. And so consequently, no one ever went
through life carrying the weight of more than several
dozen deaths on top of them.

We have death differently now. The sheer volume
of death in the global village demands it. Think how
many people had Judy Garland's death, for instance.
Hundreds of thousands. If not millions. In fact, she's
still having them—in bars where female impersonators
reign; in homes where late night movies are watched,
alone; in poster shops; in the costumes of Halloween;
in little girls' dreams down the yellow brick road.

I had a handful of those Judy Garland Deaths. I didn't
know it at the time.

Since then I've had about a couple hundred thousand
deaths, I guess. These are my deaths, in part: My
grandfather. Chips, our boxer. Obi-Wan Kenobi.
J F K. My best friend in the 5th grade, hit by a train
on her way to church. Ophelia. Tony Curtis in *Tarus
Bulba*—Yul Brynner shoots him for betraying the
Cossacks to the Poles. A bullet, right through the
shining Polish armor, straight into Tony's wavy black
haired heart—and mine. My grandmother. Princess Di.

Sydney What's-His-Name in the *Tale Of Two Cities*. All
my uncles. One of my aunts. My old friend Victor, and
then his friend, Scott. My college boyfriend Jim. The six
million who died. Three thousand on a day that started
like any other, a perfect clear September morning. And
David.

There are so, so many people in the world. All having
deaths, over and over. We are not far away, I'm
afraid, from a moment of critical mass, of geometric
progression, when we are all carrying so many deaths
that the system must collapse, like a black hole, must
just consume itself in its own weight.

I feel the irreversible heaviness, the unnatural slowness
already. Our deaths pile up on top of us. And one
day their weight makes taking a step toward a person
we love like carrying a brontosaurus on your back
while dodging across eight lanes of LA traffic. With
your teeth sunk into the dinosaur's tail to keep it from
slipping. Once it falls you will never, ever be able to
lift it up again. You will never be able to shoulder the
weight of your deaths. And move toward someone you
love.

When my brother David died he had—oh, at least a
couple thousand deaths. And he's still having them,
in all the people who loved him, and who he loved. A
remembered joke he told—a pair of shoulders shaped
like his, seen for an instant in a crowd—the most
ordinary detail of the most ordinary day—reminds us
of him...and David dies again. In those he loved.

This is the story of one of David's deaths. This is the
death of David's that was had by two redheads. This is
David's Redhaired Death.

There have been times I've let it slip back into
brownette, it's true— *(She runs her hand through her
hair.)* —and in certain light, only my hairdresser can
tell for sure. But I will always think of it as red, even

after it is gray. Of course, even after it is gray, it will still be red—at least for awhile. Now the Redhead—

*(Lights up on* MARILYN. *She lies on a bed, on white sheets, asleep. Jean moves toward the bed.)*

JEAN: —the other redhead—is a more honest redhead. Her hair is naturally the color mine is on purpose. She takes it several steps redder—brighter, but notice— *(She lightly touches the Redhead's hair.)* —no brassy highlights—no give away tones—she takes it to a shade found only on young Irish girls who live in the green hills where the deaths are still numbered in hundreds. Not hundreds of thousands.

This is the redhaired death of David's, one of many, not complete, not ever finished. Someday it will fade, like my hair, to a shade, a shadow, one lost in a crowd of shadows, like a mousy blond lost in the streets below. This is the redhaired death, the death of David's that was had by the two redheads, Marilyn and Jean— in this room, on this bed, in these arms.

David's Redhaired Death.

*(Two stage* TECHNICIANS *appear as the light changes to a kind of moonlight. The* TECHNICIANS *are tall, dark haired men.)*

*(*JEAN *leaves the bed area.)*

*(One* TECHNICIAN *begins the transformation of the bed area into the magical redhaired world—perhaps he hangs shell and shrimp colored mythic lingerie from a flying buttress or a tree branch, perhaps he spreads a luscious magenta colored duvet over the sleeping Redhead's body—or perhaps the colors are green, deep forest green—and red arrives later in the transformation.)*

*(The other* TECHNICIAN *scoops up a bit of dust from the ground, and blows it into Jean's hair. He takes a large McDonald's coke and holds it up so Jean can take a sip from*

*it— the lid is loose, some spills down her blouse. He hands her a road map, a pair of sunglasses, a credit card.)*

*(JEAN gets into her car.)*

JEAN: The road came up to meet me in Pennsylvania, then Ohio. I was on my way to the Redhead's in a royal blue 1985 Pontiac Tempest—a high seas cruiser of the highway, a boat of a car. But—as the sailors say—the water is your friend. It's the land you have to watch out for.

*(The Tempest makes hideous engine trouble sounds.)*

JEAN: I ran aground outside Chicago.

*(The Tempest makes "grinding to a halt" noises. JEAN gets out, goes around to inspect the engine.)*

JEAN: I pulled into a Texaco station, and trusted my car to the man who wears the star.

*(One of the TECHNICIANS pops the hood, and looks inside. He shakes his head, sadly.)*

JEAN: It was the transmission. Now the transmission turns out to be a closed black box, not unlike Pandora's. Once you open it up, you're stuck—there's no shutting the lid and going on. The sensible traveler, faced with transmission trouble, takes the roadside mechanic's advice and turns around and heads for home. *(She slaps the hood of the car shut, and climbs back in.)* I ignored the mechanic's warning. What did a roadside mechanic know? I was on my way to the Redhead's. The mythical, magical Redhead's. And no power on earth could have gotten me to turn around and head for home.

*(One of the TECHNICIANS holds a phone, some distance away from the stage. It rings, with a far off sound.)*

MARILYN: At a midtown Holiday Inn Hotel, a desk clerk is calling the fire department. This is the first of the calls that will trap us with David's death. There is a fire on the fourteenth floor.

JEAN: *(She puts the car in gear, continues driving. The Tempest makes unobtrusive, but odd engine noises.)* The Tempest raced strangely though the fading hills. I bought a few moments of daylight, chasing the sun west. Astronauts in space see the sun rise and set seven times a day. This is my version of *Fiddler On The Roof*, in space: *(She starts off slow, then sings VERY FAST.)* Sunrise, sunset. Sunrise, sunset. Sunrise sunset. SunriseSunset.
Sunrisesunset Sunrisesunsetsunrisesunset.
*(Pause)* Anyway, the best the Tempest could do, from a dead stop. was sunrise, sunset...period. I knew that. It didn't stop me, though. I was on my way to the Redhead's, the mythical, magical Redhead's—and when I got there, it would be wonderful.
I remembered the first time.

*(JEAN takes a step in MARILYN's direction.)*

*(MARILYN gets out of bed and walks toward JEAN. They stop several feet from each other.)*

MARILYN: Hi. You must be Jean.

JEAN: You're Marilyn.

MARILYN: Hello.

JEAN: I've heard a lot about you.

MARILYN: From Bob?

JEAN: From Bob.

MARILYN: Me too.

JEAN: Funny, you look different from the way I imagined you.

MARILYN: You too. You're a redhead.

JEAN: So are you.

MARILYN: You don't meet that many redheads.

JEAN: No, you don't.

MARILYN: Real redheads, I mean. Most redheads you meet come out of a bottle. Lady Clairol.

JEAN: L'Oreal.

*(Pause)*

MARILYN: *(Lying)* I'm a real redhead.

JEAN: *(Lying)* So am I.

JEAN/MARILYN: You can always tell.

MARILYN: One redhead to another can always tell.

JEAN: *(To the audience)* It was love at first sight. It was lots of giggling, lots of phone calls, lots of hidden picture looks across crowded rooms. We looked so special to each other. We looked so right. We each had a redhaired heart to look inside of, and see it as if it were our own hearts beating. No one could look at us the way we looked at each other.

People used to fear the redheaded woman—she had, they claimed, the power to witch a man, enchant him. As it turned out, the Redhead and I had tested out our powers on men for years. For all our lives. Now it was time to try it on an equal. *(To* MARILYN*)* Nice to finally meet you.

MARILYN: Nice to meet you.

*(*JEAN *and* MARILYN *cross the few feet between them, extend their hands and shake.* JEAN *realizes she has a French fry in her hand.)*

JEAN: Oh...I'll bet you're wondering what I'm doing with this French fry...

MARILYN: It is late when you arrive.

JEAN: No—

MARILYN: You are tired—

JEAN: Not yet—

MARILYN: You come to bed—

JEAN: *(To the audience)* A fall from a great height changes everything. Take a penny, for instance.

MARILYN: Jean— *(She sighs.)*

JEAN: If you drop one on the floor/

MARILYN: /Bob warned me about you.

JEAN: you probably don't—

MARILYN: *(Louder, insistent)* BOB WARNED ME ABOUT YOU.

*(JEAN stuffs the French fry back in her pocket, returns to MARILYN.)*

JEAN: Bob warned me about *you.*

MARILYN: He did?

JEAN: Bob's a slime.

MARILYN: Yes, he told me all about you.

JEAN: He told me about *you.*

MARILYN: Bob's a slime. I'll bet none of the things he told either of us about the other are true.

JEAN: He said be careful of Marilyn. She's a redhead.

MARILYN: He said be careful of Jean. The first time I met her, she wore a see-through blouse.

JEAN: It wasn't *really* see through.

MARILYN: *Mine was.*

*(Pause)*

JEAN: Look—it's none of my business, but Bob told me that you and he were—

MARILYN: I'm not surprised. He says that about everyone.

JEAN: Everyone?

MARILYN: Yes. The story he told about you and him and a baby grand was sublime.

JEAN: The slime. Even if he were the last man on earth, I wouldn't touch him.

MARILYN: Yes. I'd let the human race die out before I'd touch that slime.

JEAN: You know, Bob has no shame.

MARILYN: None at all. One time I had to sit there and listen to him tell the story of my conquest of a Nobel Prize winner. He had this whole story, this fantasy, and he had the nerve to tell it to someone while I was sitting right there in front of him.

JEAN: So—what happened when you denied it?

MARILYN: The more you deny it, the more the other person thinks it's true.

JEAN: Was it?

MARILYN: Yes. A completely different Nobel Prize winner, but Bob is occasionally a lucky son of a bitch.

JEAN: So—what was it like?

MARILYN: Well, if you've heard Bob's version—

JEAN: No, tell me the real one. I've always wondered what it would be like with a Nobel Prize winner.

MARILYN: So did I. In many ways, Bob's version was far superior to mine. In Bob's version, the old man performs like a boy of seventeen, has a heart attack, and dies.

JEAN: And in yours?

MARILYN: The old man remains an old man. It takes a hell of a long time to win the Nobel Prize. I put on my clothes, he calls me a cab, I go home.

JEAN: And the heart attack—

MARILYN: Three days later.

JEAN: Had nothing to do with you.

MARILYN: Well...three days is a long time, but a girl can dream, can't she? I mean, he was a very old man. I mean, come on, haven't you ever...you know, wanted to believe you could kill a man by the way you looked? Construction workers, come on, you know. You're trying to get across the street, they're throwing their lunch buckets down in front of you, their tongues are hanging out, and they all claim to know exactly what you like to do at night. You can't tell me you don't want to turn toward the one who's yelling "Hey there, Red, I could die for you, baby" —open your coat wide, and give him the good long look that buries him?

(MARILYN *opens her robe, seductively, toward* JEAN.)

(JEAN *takes a step in her direction, then hurries back to the Tempest.*)

JEAN: *(To the audience)* It is almost dark. I am beginning to wish I'd taken the mechanic's advice. But no one ever takes sound advice. In the story of Rapunzel, we focus on the Prince who makes it, on the one in a hundred who carries Rapunzel down her golden rope of hair. We forget all about the other ninety-nine guys who didn't make it. All the poor slobs who should have heeded the witch's warning, but didn't, who saw no reason why they shouldn't be the one to wrap their legs around Rapunzel's heavy plait of shining hair. And so I had faith that I would make it to the Redhead's. And that when I got there it would be wonderful.

This was our second meeting. On the way over to see her, I'd stopped at the 7-11, to get some smokes. There are no accidents, and the Redhead and I smoked the same brand.

*(A* TECHNICIAN *gives* JEAN *two packs of Camel Filters.)*

JEAN: Ever notice there's a naked man in the camel on the front of the pack?

*(*JEAN *tosses one of the packs to* MARILYN. *Along with it, at least one French fry goes sailing through the air.* JEAN *realizes she is still holding a French fry as well.)*

JEAN: Oh—I'll bet you're wondering what I'm doing with this French fry.

MARILYN: It is late when you arrive.

JEAN: No, please, not yet—

MARILYN: You are tired.

JEAN: *(To the audience)* A fall from a great height changes everything.

MARILYN: What do you think you're doing, Jean!

JEAN: Take a penny, for instance. If— *(She will continue to tell her story, under* MARILYN.*)* —/you drop one on the floor, you probably don't even bother picking it up anymore. if you drop a penny from the top of the Empire State Building, however, that penny transforms itself into the weight of—

MARILYN: /This is not the way it happens, Jean. It is late when you arrive. You are tired, you come to bed. The phone rings. THE PHONE RINGS.

*(The phone rings, far away. A* TECHNICIAN *carries the phone closer to the stage.)*

*(*JEAN *continues, falteringly.)*

JEAN: —transforms itself into the weight of a thousand or more pounds on its way to the ground.

MARILYN: At the fire department, the central dispatcher is calling for back up, for extension ladders, for special upper story crews. And in the Holiday Inn the alarms are ringing on the floor, in the hallways, in the bar, the

coffee shop, the lobby. Guests are scurrying from their
rooms, half packed suitcases under their arms.
They are flooding into the elevators. They are rushing
headlong down the stairs. They are pouring onto the
street and staring up at the flames.

*(The* TECHNICIAN *moves the phone closer, it rings
insistently.)*

MARILYN: An ambulance is called. The door to the
burning room is jammed, or barricaded, and inside
someone has started to scream.

JEAN: Ever notice there's a naked man in the camel on
the front of the pack?

MARILYN: Jean, let's get it over with.

JEAN: Here's his leg, right where the camel's leg is—I
can't believe Bob didn't show you too.

MARILYN: This just makes it harder. Let's get it behind
us, move on—

JEAN: Here's his arm—he's holding it like this— *(She
demonstrates, using her arm.)*

MARILYN: Come to bed, Jean, let's get it over with—

JEAN: And here is his— *(She indicates a large penis.)*

MARILYN: Jean I can't—

JEAN: You can't say you don't see it, Marilyn. It's the
size of a small nuclear submarine.

MARILYN: I can't. Do this. I—

JEAN: Oh. I didn't realize it was so late—you must have
other plans for dinner, I'll leave. *(She turns, and starts to
go.)*

MARILYN: NO!

JEAN: *(Pause)* No, what?

MARILYN: Jean. Please. Don't do this.

JEAN: *(Prompting* MARILYN*)* No, I don't have other plans....

MARILYN: *(Resigned)* No, I don't have other plans.

JEAN: *(Still prompting)* Do you want to go out...

MARILYN: Do you want to go out?

JEAN: And get...

MARILYN: And get...

*(*JEAN *waits.* MARILYN *gives in.)*

MARILYN: ...something to eat?

JEAN: *(Thinks about it for an instant. Lightly)* No.

MARILYN: *(Monotone, still an unwilling participant)*
You're sure? Because if you're on a diet or something, I know this great salad place, all kinds of—

JEAN: *(Seductively)* Oh, I never bother with diets, not really. If I gain a pound or two, I just instinctively stop eating for a couple days. Don't you?

MARILYN: *(Can't help laughing. She is drawn in again.)*
No. What planet are you from?

JEAN: *(They are both laughing now.)* It's just I ate already. At McDonald's. It's silly. Crazy. I have this thing about McDonald's. *(To the audience)* The Redhead never even saw it coming. A McDonald's story was not exactly the usual redhead attack. Here we were, both orchestrating the subtle ways we would prove who was the stronger redhead, the better redhead, the deadlier redhead.
But I could tell that I didn't stand a chance against the Redhead with the usual redhead array—sultry looks, unspoken promises, that sort of thing. I had seen that right away.
So I circled around back and got the drop on her. With the McDonald's story. *(To* MARILYN*)* I have this— thing—about McDonald's.

MARILYN: Tell me.

JEAN: *(As if embarrassed)* Oh, no, you don't want to know.

MARILYN: But I do.

JEAN: Not really.

MARILYN: Cross my redhaired heart and hope to—

JEAN: Redhaired heart?

MARILYN: Yes. Don't you think of it like that?

JEAN: *(To the audience)* This is the moment in the chronology of the redheads when the redhaired heart is officially carried out into the open like a 4-H Club's Nativity scene in a Christmas parade. *(To* MARILYN*)* Yes.

MARILYN: I really want to hear about this thing you have about McDonald's. Cross my redhaired heart and hope to die.

JEAN: *(As if reluctantly)* Okay. If that's what you want. *(She sits down next to* MARILYN *on the bed.)* I was at McDonald's, ordering a quarter pounder with cheese—

*(*MARILYN *kisses* JEAN's *wrist.)*

Jean: —a large coke—

*(*MARILYN *kisses the inside of* JEAN's *elbow.)*

JEAN: —and a large fry—

*(*MARILYN *kisses* JEAN's *neck.)*

JEAN: And in a midtown Holiday Inn Hotel, my brother David... *(She stops, lost, confused. She pulls away from* MARILYN, *leaps off the bed.)* NO! ...I was at McDonald's, ordering a quarter pounder with cheese, a large Coke, and a large fry, because ever since I was thirteen years old, and my parents told me I had to have a goal in life, I've had this plan.

I wanted to order the exact same thing—a quarter
pounder with cheese, a large coke, a large fry—in
Louisiana, in Mississippi, in Hawaii. In every state,
in the map I got from McDonald's marking every
Golden Arch marked town. I wanted to say the same
eleven words, pay with a five dollar bill, receive the
exact same change. Eat identical food, identically,
ritualistically—three French fries, one bite of burger,
one sip of coke. I knew in advance that the decor
would inevitably vary—Townhouse McDonald's, with
their fake exposed brick. Country Cottage McDonald's,
with rough hewn plastic stones littering the floor.
And in Missouri, they say, there is the Taj Mahal of
McDonald's—costing over a million dollars to build,
with three different theme eating areas featuring one
hundred thousand dollars worth of rare antiques, all
bolted down. And in the Dutch decorated room is a
portrait of Ronald McDonald after the school of Van
Eyk. And in another, the French room, he's painted
in a Renoir-like shimmer of light. And in the third,
he's the all male Western Ronald, sitting high in the
saddle on a brave, earth tone range. His ten gallon hat
pushed jauntily back, on his mop of bright red hair.
(To the audience) Of course, things rarely work out the
way they're planned. Here I was expecting a nice, easy
fight—while I was charming the Redhead with the
story of my life plan for McDonald's—which is a true
story, but an insane one, its insanity being the secret of
its charm—I'd be bringing up my heavy artillery on the
side. Bring the Redhead under my spell, and waste her.
Instead, the Redhead decided to get the drop on me.
If there was any hope of our avoiding a very intense,
very messy, very up and down, up and down kind of
unnatural redhair affair, after what was only the tip
of the iceberg of the McDonald's story, it was gone
as soon as the Redhead made the first move. To her
cigarettes.

(MARILYN *opens her pack of Camel Filters.*)

JEAN: It was a standard in the redhaired arsenal. I reached for mine. *(She does.)* The lighting up, while gazing into the eyes.

(JEAN *and* MARILYN *light up, gaze into each other's eyes, etc. They are like gunslingers, facing each other down.*)

JEAN: The long inhale...the longer exhale. The gauzy smoke caressing the face. The cigarette that makes the victim think she's looking across at the mysteries of Greta Garbo—who wasn't a redhead, but should have been.

(JEAN *and* MARILYN *continue to smoke and seduce.*)

JEAN: I matched the Redhead's movements. She matched mine. She was good.
She was complete. She thought she had the drop on me.
And then it happened.

JEAN/MARILYN: *(Both start speaking seductively, on the exhale)* A LITTLE CLOSER TO HEAVEN...WITH A CIGARETTE IN MY HAND... *(They look at each other, incredulously.)* A little closer to heaven with a cigarette in my hand?
Oh— *(They begin laughing.)* I don't believe it—

MARILYN: The exact same line— *(Very slow)* I don't/

JEAN: *(Very fast)* /I don't—

JEAN/MARILYN: —believe it!

JEAN: It's one of my favorite lines!/

MARILYN: /Yes, I guess Bob told you it was *my* favorite line.

JEAN: Oh, God.

MARILYN: But I don't remember using it on Bob—he must have seen me use it on someone else. The slime.

JEAN: Well who else could have told you?

MARILYN: Told me what?

JEAN: That line, told you to use my favorite line.

MARILYN: That's my favorite line.

JEAN: I don't believe it—

MARILYN: I don't believe it!

JEAN: *(To the audience)* We couldn't fucking believe it. We quickly checked to see if we were the same person. *(To* MARILYN, *as the* TECHNICIANS *make the final changes that transform the bed area into the mythical, magical redhaired world.)* I've got a younger brother, an older brother.

MARILYN: I've got a younger brother, an older brother.

JEAN: I've got a grandmother I call Nano.

MARILYN: I've got a grandmother I call Nana.

JEAN: Nana?

MARILYN: Nano...

JEAN: Well, adjusting for regional dialect differences—

MARILYN: Yes, it's exactly the same.

JEAN: I love my family.

MARILYN: I love mine too.

JEAN: I loved my family, very much, but growing up I knew I was different.

MARILYN: I loved my family, very much, but I didn't fit in.

JEAN/MARILYN: Everyday of my life I had to wear this scarlet letter that said: DO NOT PASS GO.

MARILYN: DO NOT FIT IN.

JEAN: It started fading—but it was—

JEAN/MARILYN: —too late by then.

MARILYN: It started fading too late to fit in.

JEAN: *(Pause. They both pull back a bit, overwhelmed.)* Spooky, huh?

MARILYN: Coincidence. Coincidence, that's all it is, it's just—

JEAN: I have been waiting all my life to recognize someone the way I recognize myself.

MARILYN: The way I recognize you.

JEAN: The way I recognize you.

MARILYN: Here's what I've done while I've been waiting. Here's what I've been doing while I've been hunting you: I love Sam Shepard's plays. I wear Ralph Lauren perfume. I eat Chinese food. I prefer blue ink over black, black clothing over blue. There are the facts of how I've hunted you.

JEAN: Me too. And we both smoke camel filters.

MARILYN: Which will be very convenient, when one or the other of us runs out.

JEAN: I'm really trying to quit.

MARILYN: Who isn't? I'll bet every pack of Camel Filters that's sold is bought by a Camel Filter smoker who wants to quit.

*(JEAN and MARILYN smoke.)*

JEAN: Once I fell in love with a man I thought I recognized.

MARILYN: I must have met that man a hundred times.

JEAN: But the more familiar he looks over dinner, the better the chances are he'll be almost unrecognizable by midnight.

MARILYN: A total stranger by three a.m.

JEAN: A bad memory by morning.

MARILYN: You think you recognize him every time, but it turns out he doesn't want anything interesting—

MARILYN: Or remarkable—

JEAN: —or enduring from you.

MARILYN: It turns out, that if most men were women, other men would call them—

JEAN/MARILYN: Whores.

JEAN: You'd think a redhead would be immune.

MARILYN: But even a redhead can't help going back for more.

JEAN: *(A sigh of longing)* Men.

MARILYN: All those men.

JEAN: So what if they're whores—the things you can find out from them!

MARILYN: Amazing, isn't it?

JEAN: And for a redhead, so goddamn easy.

MARILYN: Like taking candy from a baby.

JEAN: All those men.

MARILYN: You know, it's funny, but I don't think any of them were ever redheads.

JEAN: I wonder why.

MARILYN: I never consciously ruled out redheads.

JEAN: Just aren't that many of them around.

MARILYN: Maybe only redhaired girls grow up to be redheads. I remember my father telling my brothers, when we were little: You can take out all the flashy blondes you want, do what you want with them in the back seat of the car. But when you marry—marry mousy brown.

JEAN: Your father really said that?

MARILYN: But what do you do with the redheads,
I wanted to ask him. He never said, but he knew.
Redhaired girls are supposed to fade into brown!
That's where all the little redhaired boys are, Jean.
Every one of them's faded into marrying brown.

JEAN: But not us.

MARILYN: Not us.

JEAN: Not yet.

MARILYN: If I have one life to live—

JEAN: Let me live it as a redhead.

MARILYN: Let me make it to the drugstore before the
roots start to show.

JEAN: Let me chose a soft, natural, but vibrant color.

MARILYN: With no brassy highlights, no give-away
tones.

JEAN: Lead me not into temptation by colors called—
*(Painful to say)* Racy Spiced Wine.

MARILYN: Red Hot Rose.

JEAN: Fuchsia Plum.

MARILYN: I almost bought some Fuchsia Plum the
other day.

JEAN: Me too!

MARILYN: I took it from the shelf. I had it in my hand!

JEAN: I couldn't do it. I chickened out.

MARILYN: So much for your brave, true redhaired
heart, I said.

JEAN: But if we went in together—

MARILYN: The two of us together—

JEAN: The redhaired badge of courage—

MARILYN: We'd be strong enough together.

JEAN: We'd buy all the Fuchsia Plum they had. To hell with "only your hairdresser knows for sure."

MARILYN: To hell with 'em all! Let 'em know, the minute we walk into a room. Our hair dyed the exact same shade.

JEAN: Double your redhead pleasure.

MARILYN: Double your redhaired fun.

JEAN: And be twins.

JEAN/MARILYN: *(They lock arms.)* PRESENTING— FOR ONE LIFE ONLY—THE SWEET AND FUNNY REDHAIRED TWINS!!!!! *(They do a little vaudeville bit, kicking and swaying.)*
They dye their hair alike
They smoke alike
They love alike
They joke alike
You could lose your miiiiiiiind—

*(The phone rings.)*

*(MARILYN pulls away from JEAN, leaving her in the middle of the big kick.)*

JEAN: When redheads—are two of a kind! When redheads are—

MARILYN: That was just a game.

JEAN: It was a real game.

*(The phone continues to ring.)*

MARILYN: Maybe to you.

JEAN: It was real.

MARILYN: Not anymore.

JEAN: It was a real game and we loved to play it. No matter how many times the phone rings, we loved to play that game.

MARILYN: *(The phone continues to ring, as the technician brings it almost to the edge of the stage.)* The calls are getting closer, tacking Jean down. They are getting a bead on her from the imprint on the MasterCard David used when he checked in to the hotel. A computer somewhere in Atlanta is printing out a phone number and an address. *(She moves toward the bed area.)* It is late when you arrive.

JEAN: It wasn't a game—

MARILYN: You are tired—

JEAN: You wanted this. You wanted a sister to stand up for you when your brothers teased you.

MARILYN: You come to bed—

JEAN: *(She grabs MARILYN, whispers in her ear.)* You loved your family, your family loved you, but right there at the beginning, it was always there—the raven blackhaired family wheeling along the baby carriage filled with red hair.

MARILYN: *(Insistently)* It is late when you arrive.

JEAN: "You can't be our little sister, our little sister has black hair."

MARILYN: *(Still trying)* You are tired, you come to bed.

JEAN: "Somebody stole our real little sister and gave us a flame head. A carrot top."

MARILYN: *(Can't help joining in)* "A marmalade brain."

JEAN: "Scarlet O'Heada—"

MARILYN: "We're gonna trade you in an' get our real sister back."

JEAN: My brother Jim said there was just one chance.

MARILYN: To be like them.

JEAN: To finally fit in.

MARILYN: If I cut it all off, all the way down, when it grew back in, it'd grow in black.

JEAN: I asked my brother David, but he just laughed. Even if I pulled it out by the roots, he said, it still wouldn't grow in black.

MARILYN: I had all this lovely, long golden red hair. Everybody was always telling my mother it would be a tragedy to cut it. It would be a crime to wear it short.

JEAN: I wasn't strong enough, but my brother Jim said he would help me do it. We went into my bedroom, and Jim locked the door. He had me hold onto the doorknob, and then he took a big handful of my hair. He started pulling. It hurt. It burned. I screamed but he wouldn't stop. David pounded on the door, he yelled for Jim to stop. Jim had me by the hair, he was dragging me across the room, my hair started ripping out. I grabbed a hanger from the closet and swung it at Jim as hard as I could. It was an accident, really.

(JEAN *and* MARILYN *are giggling together.*)

JEAN: It caught him through the lip. I had him on the hook of the hanger like a big blackhaired fish. (*She stops laughing.*) And then the door gave way. David rushed in, my father right behind him, he took one look at Jim's lip, and came at me with his belt. But David wouldn't let him touch me.
I cried all night and David held me. He said "I'm going to hold you until it's all right." And in the morning, when he let go of me, it was.
And when it grew back in—

MARILYN: It didn't grow in black.

JEAN: No. It didn't grow in black. But it never looked the same.

(JEAN *and* MARILYN *are touching each other's hair, stroking it softly.*)

JEAN: But if I'd had a redhaired sister—

MARILYN: *(Whispering)* A redhaired sister...I always wanted a redhaired sister...

JEAN: *(Whispering)* All my own.

*(JEAN and MARILYN continue to touch and caress, but they don't kiss. They continue until the phone rings.)*

MARILYN: *(Dreamy)* Do you believe in miracles, Jean?

JEAN: I believe in McDonald's.

MARILYN: You've got a point. McDonald's is not exactly likely. Given all the possibilities for life on earth, McDonald's is not what you'd expect.
Do you think, on the scale of things, that what is happening to us is more probable than McDonald's, or less?

JEAN: *(To the audience, as they embrace, over the Redhead's shoulder.)* The Redhead couldn't believe what was happening to her. Neither could I. We were hypnotized, but wide awake at the same time. No matter what I said, it was right. No matter what the Redhead did, it was perfect. This was love—infinite, redhead, and pure. There were no odd angles, no extra digits, this was it. This was the enchanted redhead world where no matter what story I told, it was always the McDonald's story, and the McDonald's story was anything I goddamn wanted it to be.
I held the Redhead close. It was...confusing...I wanted to hold her, to do nothing but hold her, to not stop holding her, but when we touched, her skin was dry, and rough, like sandpaper, she scraped against my skin. It was confusing...but it was also wonderful. It was part of the redhead world, wasn't it? *(To MARILYN)* Marilyn, I—

MARILYN: Yes?

JEAN: Marilyn, I want to—

MARILYN: Yes?

JEAN: Marilyn, I—

MARILYN: Say it, Jean.

JEAN: *(About to kiss* MARILYN*)* Marilyn, I—

*(The phone rings, as the* TECHNICIAN *brings it to the edge of the stage.)*

*(*JEAN *breaks away from* MARILYN, *returns to the Tempest.)*

JEAN: *(To the audience)* I am a hundred miles away from the Redhead's, on the outskirts of Madison when it happens.

MARILYN: The fire has grown, engulfing the hotel room, billowing out from it like a giant red flare. The ladder has been extended, a fireman smashes the flames back with a stream of water and leans in through the shattered window. He extends his hand. The man in the room looks at him, confused, pushes him aside, and goes out the window. He reaches the ground in less time than it takes to say, less time than it takes to tell.

*(The phone rings again as the* TECHNICIAN *moves it on to the stage.)*

JEAN: A call makes its way to my mother and father within an hour. They are listed as credit references on my brother's MasterCard.

*(A* TECHNICIAN *hands* JEAN *a gift-wrapped package as she steps out of the Tempest.)*

MARILYN: You know what I want?

*(*MARILYN *lights up a cigarette, offers one to* JEAN.*)*

JEAN: This was our third time together. Things were happening fast, even for redheads. And redheads like things fast. It's not how long you make it—it's how you make it long. *(She takes the cigarette.)*

MARILYN: I want a cigarette that shuts off at exactly the right instant. I want a Camel Filter that knows.

*(JEAN surprises MARILYN with the gift. MARILYN opens it, and takes out a sexy negligee. MARILYN puts it on.)*

JEAN: I do too. All the things you're thinking, I'm thinking too. I am thinking how you smell, I am thinking that I also wear Ralph Lauren's perfume. I am thinking I like Sam Shepard, Chinese Food, prefer blue ink to black, black clothing over blue. I am thinking about what touching you will do. I am thinking we are in trouble, or in Paradise. *(To the audience)* Who had time to choose? *(To MARILYN, as she comes out to model the negligee.)* I love you.

MARILYN: I love you.

*(JEAN and MARILYN touch each other's hair, then stop.)*

MARILYN: Well. What do you think we should do about this?

JEAN: We could call up Bob. He's spreading some very interesting rumors about us.

MARILYN: We could call up Bob, ask him what he's been saying about us, and then do it.

JEAN/MARILYN: He's such a slime.

JEAN: It'd almost be worth it just to do it, just so we could call him up and thank him for introducing us. Rub it in that we're doing it with each other and not with him.

MARILYN: Yes. It's the kind of thing that could kill a slime like Bob.

JEAN: This is getting confusing, Marilyn.

MARILYN: I know.

JEAN: Really, really confusing.

MARILYN: I know.

JEAN: I'm not used to things like this being confusing.

MARILYN: No, not for a redhead.

JEAN: Never for a redhead.

MARILYN: It wasn't even all that confusing when I was with that woman before.

JEAN: It didn't sound confusing.

MARILYN: It wasn't. It was really fun. Good, clean school girl fun.

JEAN: I remember when everything was good clean school girl fun.

MARILYN: Yes.

JEAN: Where I went to school, it was just thought of as part of the liberal arts degree. Since then, I really haven't thought about it at all.

MARILYN: I thought it would be sweet, and funny. And easy. It's always been easy before, right?

JEAN: Always. Even when it looked like love.

JEAN/MARILYN: It always looked like love.

JEAN: But this is hard.

MARILYN: And it is love.

JEAN: And it's confusing.

MARILYN: *(She sighs.)* Maybe we should have done it before...before we got to be twins.

JEAN: I wonder why we didn't think of it then.

MARILYN: Just think, it'd be out of the way, we could get on with being the redheads.

JEAN: But we'll still be the redheads after, won't we?

MARILYN: Of course.

JEAN: I mean, even after it's—over?

MARILYN: Jean—who says it's ever going to be over?

JEAN: Oh.

*(Beat.* JEAN *and* MARILYN *pull away from each other by a fraction of an inch.)*

JEAN: *(To the audience)* We had reached a critical impasse in the redhaired affair.

MARILYN: *(Sighing)* Do you know what life is like, Jean?

JEAN: I know what McDonald's is like.

MARILYN: This can't go on, Jean.

JEAN: I know.

MARILYN: We have to move on—

JEAN: I know.

MARILYN: Next time.

JEAN: All right.

MARILYN: Cross your redhaired heart?

JEAN: Cross my redhaired heart. I promise. Next time.

*(*JEAN *returns to the Tempest, as* MARILYN *lies down in her bed. She sleeps.)*

JEAN: *(To the audience)* I was almost at the Redhead's. Just another thirty or forty miles. I had not taken the mechanics advice and I had made it. Not only that, but I was making it in record redhead to redhead time.

*(The* TECHNICIAN *moves the phone to the Redhead's bedside table. The phone rings, at the Redhead's.)*

JEAN: The Redhead is a heavy sleeper, the Redhead is a deep, unreachable dream. My mother lets it ring and ring and ring.

*(The ringing stops.)*

JEAN: An hour later, she'll have to make the call again.
But for the moment, for an hour, David's death has
been delayed.
And I am racing toward it. Eighty-five, ninety miles
an hour. How did the crippled Tempest manage such
speeds? Like a horse in the Black Stallion series, whose
leg has been shattered in the crush of flying hooves at
the starting gate, and runs to the finish line on heart
alone.

*(The Tempest makes valiant transmission dying noises.)*

JEAN: I had worn the transmission down to the bone,
the way the princess in the fairy tale wore out three
pairs of stone shoes and broke three stone walking
sticks on her way to her true love. She also sucked
three stone loaves down to pebbles. I went to...
McDonald's.

*(The TECHNICIANS perform the duties of McDonald's
employees at a drive-thru. They load a McDonald's bag for
JEAN, and hand it to her.)*

JEAN: I ordered a quarter pounder with cheese, a
large coke, and a large fry. I was ten miles from the
Redhead's, but I needed that last sacred pit stop. When
your transmission is shot, and reverse is gone, the
drive-through is a blessing for the traveler who can not
turn back.

*(The Tempest races on for an instant, then sputters to a halt,
and dies. JEAN leaves the Tempest.)*

*(JEAN opens the bag, takes out a French fry, and places it on
the ground behind her. She leaves a trail of French fries, as
she arrives at the Redhead's.)*

JEAN: I arrived at the Redhead's.
This was it. We had it all mapped out. We had a double
redhead plan. Cross our redhaired hearts. We had
agreed.

(JEAN *bends down, and kisses* MARILYN *lightly on the forehead.* MARILYN *wakes, reaches out to* JEAN, JEAN *reaches to embrace her. They both realize* JEAN *has a French fry in her hand.*)

JEAN: Oh—I'll bet you're wondering what I'm doing with this French fry.

MARILYN: As a matter of fact, I am.

JEAN: *(To the audience)* A fall from a great height changes everything.

MARILYN: Stop it Jean—there's no where else to go, Jean—JEAN!

JEAN: Take a penny for instance. If you drop one on the floor, you probably don't even bother picking it up anymore.

MARILYN: You are tired, you come to bed.

JEAN: If you drop a penny from the top of the Empire State Building, however—

MARILYN: You do not tell this story. It is too late. You come to bed. The phone rings.

JEAN: *(To* MARILYN, *triumphant)* But the phone rings *after* I come to bed. It is late when I arrive, I come to bed, and the phone rings *after* I come to bed, right?

MARILYN: Right, but—

JEAN: No buts. Here we go.
A fall from a great height changes everything. If you drop a penny from the top of the Empire State building, that penny transforms itself into the weight of a thousand or more pounds on its way to the ground. On a good day, not too much wind, the penny will be embedded a good foot into the concrete, straight down. If you drop a woman from the top of the Empire State Building, however—

MARILYN: No.

JEAN: No what?

MARILYN: It's not your story.

JEAN: Maybe I didn't start it well enough. All right.
I'll start it again. A FALL FROM A GREAT HEIGHT
CHANGES—

MARILYN: It's not your story! So it doesn't matter how
you start it or if you finish it. The phone rings. Come to
bed.

JEAN: I was at McDonald's—

MARILYN: You do not tell a McDonald's story! It is late,
you are tired, you come to bed. The phone rings.

JEAN: If the phone hadn't rung, I might have told it.

MARILYN: You didn't.

JEAN: I meant to. I meant to tell you the most
magnificent McDonald's story of them all. And maybe
it would have taken forever to tell.
Maybe, with the laughing, and the holding, and the
smoking, I could have made the McDonald's story last
until the end of time. Told it until there was only you
and me and the McDonald's story. The story of each of
the billions sold. You and me in each other's arms.
I ask you—one redhead to another—can it be done?

MARILYN: No.

JEAN: I think you're lying. I think that in a world, a
parallel redhead world where the McDonald's story is
always being told, the phone doesn't ring. Maybe there
are no phones. Maybe Alexander Graham Bell was
dropped on his head as an infant or something, I don't
know. But in that world, as long as the McDonald's
story is being told, David is still alive.

MARILYN: It is late when you arrive.

JEAN: No.

MARILYN: You come to bed.

JEAN: *(To the audience, desperately, she returns to the Tempest.)* I was at McDonald's, you see, and I'd had all this car trouble. Radiator, water pump, thermostat, it was coming every fifty miles or so—

MARILYN: *(She's had enough.)* Jesus Fucking Christ—who the hell do you think you are, Jean!

JEAN: —but nothing my credit card and I couldn't handle. Then the transmission started acting up outside Chicago.

MARILYN: You've got French fries all over my room—

JEAN: I should have turned around and headed home—

MARILYN: —you change the subject every thirty seconds or so—

JEAN: —any sane person would have. I would have, but noooooooooooo—

MARILYN: And this fucking negligee—

JEAN: I was on my way to the Redhead's. The mythical, magical Redhead's. I'll be safe if I can just make it to the Redhead's.

MARILYN: —don't let me get started on this fucking negligee, I'm warning you—

JEAN: You never loved me.

MARILYN: OH FUCK OFF. *(Pause)* I did love you. *(Pause. Gently)* Once I fell in love with a redhead. *(She reaches out her hand to* JEAN.*)* Once I looked at her. And when she looked at me, we were both the double redheads, the most powerful woman in the world. The Redhead seen by the redhead seeing the Redhead. If we had wanted, we could have been the redhaired death of the world.

JEAN: *(Crying)* Then why didn't it work, why?

MARILYN: It is late when you arrive. You are laying a trail of French fries up to my bed. *(She can't help a little smile.)* I did love you. You know I loved you.

*(MARILYN gets back into bed, as JEAN takes another French fry out of the bag, slowly puts it down. She arrives at the Redhead's, as before, and wakes her, as before.)*

JEAN: Oh. I bet you're wondering what I'm doing with this French fry?

MARILYN: Well, as a matter of fact I am.

JEAN: Isn't it obvious?

MARILYN: No.

JEAN: I'm leaving a trail so I can find my way back to the Tempest.

MARILYN: Something's happened to the Tempest—

JEAN: Yes. *(She is laying down more French fries around the bed.)* It's tragic. *(She plops down on the bed.)* It's the transmission.

MARILYN: I'm sorry. What is the transmission, really?

JEAN: I have no idea. Except it's gone.

MARILYN: Where did you have to leave the car?

JEAN: Two blocks. Two blocks, and I would have made it. It could be worse. If it had happened out on the highway, I would never have had enough French fries.

MARILYN: Oh, Jean, I'm sorry.

JEAN: Well, anyway, I'm here.

*(Pause)*

MARILYN: Jean—you've been crying.

JEAN: It was a very difficult parting. *(Pause)* I'll tell you all about it in the morning. *(Pause)* So. Anyway. I got here.

*(Pause)*

MARILYN: Yes.

JEAN: I've missed you.

MARILYN: I've missed you.

*(JEAN and MARILYN start to really kiss, but quickly shift to fast pecks on the cheek. Nervously, stalling:)*

MARILYN: So. You made good time, though?

JEAN: Yes. All things considered.

*(JEAN and MARILYN attempt to kiss and embrace again, but back off shyly again.)*

MARILYN: You...hungry?

JEAN: Well, I stopped at—

MARILYN: Oh, right—

JEAN/MARILYN: McDonald's.

*(Pause. JEAN and MARILYN try to kiss again.)*

JEAN: But if *you're* hungry—

MARILYN: No, not really, I— *(She leaps out of bed.)* THIS IS MAKING ME CRAZY!

JEAN: The sweet and funny twins lose their minds. Over nothing, really.

MARILYN: We agreed—

JEAN: I know. No more dancing around it.

MARILYN: No more talking it to death.

JEAN: No more talk. Action!

MARILYN: We agreed. I am not seducing you. You are not seducing me. We are both in this together.

JEAN/MARILYN: We both get to be the redhead.

MARILYN: I am not going to wait for you to kiss me. You are not going to wait for me to kiss you.

JEAN: All right.

MARILYN: Okay.

(JEAN *and* MARILYN *both wait. They cannot keep a straight face after a moment or two.*)

JEAN: What are you waiting for Marilyn?????

MARILYN: What are you waiting for, Jean????????

JEAN: Marilyn?

MARILYN: Jean?

JEAN: I'm not the one waiting.

MARILYN: Well it's certainly not me.

JEAN: I think you're waiting...

MARILYN: Not me...

(JEAN *and* MARILYN *are playing cat and mouse on the bed.*)

JEAN: You were too—

MARILYN: No, you were the one waiting—

JEAN: I saw you waiting...I definitely saw you waiting... *(To the audience)* We didn't know it, of course, but we were waiting. For the phone to ring.

MARILYN: You are really asking for it.

(MARILYN *starts tickling* JEAN. JEAN *tickles back.*)

JEAN: Who me?

MARILYN: Yes, you! *(She tickles* JEAN *more aggressively.)* Come here—

(MARILYN *grabs* JEAN, *they kiss for an instant on the lips,* JEAN *pulls back.*)

JEAN: You promise we'll still be the redheads?

MARILYN: I promise.

JEAN: No matter what?

MARILYN: We'll be the redheads forever. No matter what.

(JEAN *and* MARILYN *come together, a long true kiss. The phone rings, they explode into laughter.*)

MARILYN: Oh, no.

(JEAN *and* MARILYN *are laughing too hard to continue the kiss. They flop on their backs, giggling.*)

MARILYN: Should I answer it, or let it ring? Maybe it'll stop.

JEAN: Maybe, if we just ignore it—

MARILYN: Go back to where we were—

JEAN: Now, where were we—

(JEAN *and* MARILYN *try to embrace and kiss again, but the phone keeps ringing, and they're laughing too hard.*)

JEAN: You might as well get it. Maybe it's Bob, with sex tips for girls.

MARILYN: *(She crawls toward the phone.)* How CAN you bring up Bob at a time like this! *(Answering the phone)* Hello?

JEAN: *(Sudden light change—spotlight on* JEAN.*)* And so David's Redhaired Death begins like this.

*(Blackout)*

END OF ACT ONE

# ACT TWO

MARILYN: (JEAN *lies on the bed, as at the end of* ACT ONE. MARILYN *moves downstage, addressing the Audience.)* A fall from a great height changes everything.

If you drop a penny from the top of the Empire State building, that penny transforms itself into the weight of a thousand or more pounds on its way to the ground. On a good day, not too much wind, the penny will be embedded a good foot into the concrete, straight down. If you drop a woman from the top of the Empire State Building, however, she is transformed into that famous picture that appeared in *Look*. She is lovely, and young, and perfectly dressed in a trim suit. Her blonde hair flows gently in waves that frame an angelic face. She is wearing gloves, but her shoes are gone, as if she has only just kicked them off before falling into what looks to be a deep, soft, rich feather bed. She lies there, an innocent, peaceful smile on her face, like an exhausted child who has succumbed to sleep the instant she hit the bed, too tired to pull the covers over her, too weary to squirm and disturb the perfect impression she has made on the satin coverlet—each line leading into the valley that cradles her body is clean, sharp, distinct. The photographer must have caught her in the instant after she lay down to sleep—in a moment, of course, the feather bed will flatten out, the satin—a dark, silky satin that shines where it catches the light—the satin will smooth out again, all the lines will be erased.

But the caption under the picture reads: "A Tragic Suicide". The soft, bright feather bed beneath the beautiful girl is in fact the crumpled roof of a Dodge. And they can carry the broken girl's body away, the photographer can take his prize and go on home. But the imprint of the body on the roof of the Dodge will remain.

I saw that picture for the first time in my pediatrician's waiting room, I was in for a tetanus shot. I was eight or nine years old. Later the photograph turned up in a collection of "The Best From Look" that we kept on our coffee table. I could look at that picture for hours. She was so beautiful. She was as lovely as Snow White, as Sleeping Beauty—lovelier than both of them rolled together. But there was a catch. She would sleep, and there would be no prince. She was sleeping for no one. It would be forever wasted sleep.

I knew that she must have done it for love, but I was too young to really care. No, what bothered me was the Dodge. What I thought about while I looked at that picture was the moment after the picture was taken. When the owner of the Dodge returned.

I imagine the man, with his family—a family like our family, his nicely dressed wife, his three spoiled children, just down from a trip up the Empire State Building. The children are fighting about who will sit in the middle this time, I sat in the middle last time. Their father herds them along, he is in a hurry, worried about the meter. They have wasted too much time at the souvenir stand, parking tickets are expensive, do his children think money grows on trees? They round the corner, and come upon the place where they have parked their car. It takes several seconds for them to realize that they are looking at their Dodge.

And I wondered, too, just how romantic the photograph would have been if the family had not

been at the souvenir stand so long. If they had been
all loaded up and ready to go, the children squirming
and elbowing each other in the back seat, their father
checking a road map in the front. If they had come
between a falling body and the ground.
The world is full of things that are falling. *(She returns
to the bed, touches the phone.)* It was Jean's mother on the
line.

*(MARILYN moves away from the bed. MARILYN uses a
controlled, blank tone for JEAN's mother and father, no color,
only calm, relentless pain. JEAN builds in terror and loss.)*

JEAN: *(Sitting up)* Mom? What's wrong—

MARILYN: Is Marilyn with you?

JEAN: Yes, why? What's—

MARILYN: Jean, it's David.

JEAN: What's wrong.

MARILYN: There's been a...accident.

JEAN: No.

MARILYN: Honey, he's...Jean, he's dead.

JEAN: Mom—

MARILYN: We don't know really how it happened,
we're all in...shock, they say.

JEAN: No.

MARILYN: *(Pause)* Marilyn is with you?

JEAN: Yes.

MARILYN: Good. That's good.

JEAN: Where's Dad?

MARILYN: Right here.

JEAN: Can I talk to him?

MARILYN: Yes.

JEAN: *(Pause)* I love you mom—

MARILYN: *(Cutting her off)* I love you too so very, very much— *(As* MARILYN, *to the audience)* Jean's mother cannot go on. She has no right, she knows, to have gotten this far.

JEAN: Daddy?

MARILYN: "We want you to know how much we love you" Jean's father says, in half a voice.

JEAN: I know, I know. Daddy I wish I was with you, I—

MARILYN: I know. We've already made the reservation—there's a flight that will get you here a little after noon. Leaves at six thirty your time. Can your friend Marilyn drive you?

JEAN: Yes.

MARILYN: Good. That's good.

JEAN: *(She begins to get hysterical.)* But the Tempest—I can't leave the Tempest, the transmission—

MARILYN: What?

JEAN: I had to leave the Tempest on the road, it—it—

MARILYN: Don't worry about the car right now, honey.

JEAN: Okay, Daddy, okay.

MARILYN: Sweetheart?

JEAN: Yes?

MARILYN: I love you.

JEAN: I love you Daddy. Daddy— *(She begins to break.)*

MARILYN: I have to see about your mother, she—

JEAN: *(Keeping it in)* Okay.

MARILYN: You'll be all right?

JEAN: Yes.

MARILYN: I hate you being up there all alone, honey.

JEAN: I'll be home tomorrow, I'll be home.

MARILYN: Tomorrow. Yes. If we can just make it through—

JEAN: Daddy—Daddy— *(It comes rushing at her again.)* —how can this be happening to us—

MARILYN: You try and get some sleep.

JEAN: This can't be happening—

MARILYN: Sweetheart I love you.

JEAN: Daddy it can't be happening—

MARILYN: We've got to call Jim still, sweetheart.

JEAN: *(Pause. She holds it in again.)* Okay.

MARILYN: You try and get some sleep.

JEAN: I will.

MARILYN: You call us tonight if you need to, no matter how late—

JEAN: Okay.

MARILYN: All right?

JEAN: I will.

MARILYN: Tomorrow when we're all together we can—

JEAN: Yes, you're right. You're right.

MARILYN: Your friend Marilyn, she'll take care of you.

JEAN: Yes.

MARILYN: Good.

JEAN: Daddy? *(Wrenched out of her)* Do you want me to call Jim?

MARILYN: *(Pause)* No, sweetheart.

JEAN: Because I will if—

MARILYN: "No" says Jean's father, and the weight of his son's death, the weight of the death multiplying

itself like a tidal wave, sweeping up the force of
David's death as it hits his daughter Jean, the death
it will be in five minutes when it strikes his son Jim—
"No", her father says, and the weight pushes his head
down under the waves, and holds it there.

(JEAN *begins to cry—she leaps off the bed, bolting for escape,*
MARILYN *grabs her and holds her while she sobs.)*

MARILYN: Jean—what's wrong—Jean—

JEAN: I can't—I can't—

MARILYN: Tell me what's wrong-

JEAN: No, I just can't. It's so sad.

MARILYN: I'm here, Jean. Tell me what's happened—

JEAN: So terribly sad.

MARILYN: You have to tell me, Jean.

JEAN: It's not fair, it's not fair, he can't be dead, he can't
be dead—

MARILYN: Oh, Jean—

JEAN: Make it all right. Make it go away.

MARILYN: I'll take care of you.

JEAN: Hold me.

MARILYN: I'm holding you.

JEAN: Tighter.

MARILYN: I'll take care of you.

JEAN: Make it all right.

MARILYN: I promise. I'll make it go away.

(MARILYN *is rocking* JEAN *in her arms, stroking her hair
and comforting her.* JEAN *is quiet for only a few moments.)*

JEAN: You shouldn't have promised me that, Marilyn.

MARILYN: I meant it.

JEAN: All the same. You shouldn't promise something if you don't really know what it means.

MARILYN: I tried to take care of you. I meant it.

JEAN: You meant it, but— *(She shrugs.)* You couldn't even get me to the airport the next morning on time.

MARILYN: That's not true.

JEAN: I wanted to go to the airport right away, but you said there was plenty of time—

MARILYN: That's not how it happened!

JEAN: Didn't you say the plane wasn't for hours? Didn't you say that?

MARILYN: Yes, but—

JEAN: I wanted to go, but you wouldn't take me.

MARILYN: That's not how it happened! You wanted me to hold you, so I held you. You fell asleep, in my arms. I woke you up in plenty of time. YOU TOLD ME TO HOLD YOU!

JEAN: No. I told you *not* to hold me.
I told you you could take me to the airport right away, or you could hold me. But if you held me, I wouldn't stop crying until you made it all right.
You were warned.

MARILYN: I held you anyway.
I held you, and you cried all night, even after you fell asleep. I didn't think a person could cry in their sleep like that. *(Almost yelling)* I didn't hold you so you could keep on crying, Jean. I held you because I wanted you to stop.

JEAN: I can't get free, Marilyn. I can't get out from under this one. I can't—

MARILYN: *(Under* JEAN*)* It is late when you arrive, you are tired—

JEAN: I know you want me to be the person who gets out from under it—

MARILYN: *(Under* JEAN*)* —you come to bed, the phone rings, and I hold you. I hold you all night, and in the morning—in the morning—

JEAN: —you want me to be the person who can carry it on top of me. But I can't.

MARILYN: I woke you up in plenty of time.

*(*JEAN *lies down with her head on a pillow in* MARILYN's *lap.* MARILYN *hands* JEAN *a Kleenex.)*

MARILYN: Here—

JEAN: *(Taking it, she dries her face, blows her nose, and puts her hand on the pillow.)* Your pillow—I've gotten it all wet—

MARILYN: Don't worry about it.

JEAN: What time is it?

MARILYN: A little before five.

JEAN: Good.

MARILYN: You feel okay?

JEAN: I don't know. Sort of like I'm in a dream. You know what I want?

MARILYN: Here—

*(*MARILYN *gives* JEAN *her cigarette, they share it.)*

JEAN: Before breakfast. Bad sign.

MARILYN: We'll survive.
There's time if you want to take a shower, but you'll have to get up now.

JEAN: No. I just want to stay here for a minute, okay?

MARILYN: Okay, sure.

JEAN: *(Silence, while they smoke.)* They taste the same.

MARILYN: What?

JEAN: Camel Filters. They still taste the same.

MARILYN: Oh.

JEAN: They taste terrible. Let's switch to a better brand, okay? Shermans or Dunhills, okay?

MARILYN: Okay.

JEAN: Okay.
It's such a crazy dream. You know what I want?

MARILYN: What?

JEAN: I want to watch T V.

MARILYN: Okay.

(MARILYN *gets up to turn on the T V*, JEAN *pulls her back down beside her.*)

JEAN: No, don't go.

MARILYN: Okay, but—

JEAN: Don't go.

MARILYN: I said I won't.

JEAN: Okay. All right. I'm sorry.

MARILYN: Don't be silly, about what?

JEAN: *(Starting to cry)* I just wondered what it would be like, you know, to watch T V in a dream.

MARILYN: *(Holding her)* It's all right, Jean, it's all right.

JEAN: *(Crying)* I never watch T V in my dreams.

MARILYN: Oh, right, sure, just public television, right? That's what they all say. A little Discovery Channel, occasionally C N N, but other than that the T V stays off in my dreams—

JEAN: Don't—don't make me laugh.

MARILYN: You started it.

(MARILYN *gives* JEAN *a hug.*)

JEAN: Just so you'd think I was being brave.

MARILYN: Aren't you?

JEAN: No. I'm just trying to keep sitting here a little longer.

MARILYN: Plenty of time.

JEAN: Yes, you're right. There'll be plenty of time from now on to watch T V in a dream.

MARILYN: I'll get us some coffee—

(MARILYN *starts to get up,* JEAN *pulls her down again.*)

JEAN: No, don't leave me—

MARILYN: Jean, come on. You'll feel better after you have a—

JEAN: *(Fiercely)* I don't want to feel better. Okay?

MARILYN: No.

JEAN: You can't say no to me—my brother's dead, I get anything I want. MY BROTHER'S DEAD AND I GET ANYTHING I WANT.

MARILYN: Okay, Jean, okay. I'm sorry.

JEAN: I'm sorry.

MARILYN: It's okay.

JEAN: I'm sorry.

MARILYN: It's okay, Jean. It's okay. *(Pause)* Jean, you can stay right here another few minutes, it's okay, but I have to go warm up the car. Okay?

JEAN: No.

MARILYN: All right, then we'll get your things and go out together, we'll sit in the car together, okay?

JEAN: No.

MARILYN: Your father's going to be there waiting, if we don't leave soon—Jean, he thinks you're coming home today, he—

JEAN: Then call him! Call him and tell him I can't come! Call him and tell him I'll be there tomorrow, tell him... tell him I just can't come.

MARILYN: I can't do that.

JEAN: Of course you can. I can't leave until I've gotten the Tempest off the road, now can I? He'll understand.

MARILYN: Jean, I'll take care of that for you—

JEAN: You don't know where it is—

MARILYN: You'll show me on the way to the airport—

JEAN: You don't know what's wrong with it—

MARILYN: So I'll take it to someone who does—

JEAN: You don't know how to drive it right—

MARILYN: *(Desperate whisper)* It's just a car, Jean. It's just...a...car. Come on—

JEAN: *(Exploding)* DON'T YOU KNOW WHAT IT'S GOING TO BE LIKE THERE? Oh, sure, it's bad here, but there—David's death is going to be everywhere. Everywhere I look, everything I touch...I'll sit there with my parents, with my brother Jim, we'll sit at the kitchen table and say things to each other but all we'll really be doing is screaming WHERE'S DAVID. WHY ISN'T HE HERE! Why doesn't he drive up in his car, why doesn't the door open, why doesn't David come walking in. We don't get together much, the way we're all spread out, but at least at a time like this you'd think your brother David would be here. We're a family and we don't get together much, but when it matters, we are all here. Why is David so late? I'm not going, Marilyn. If you love me, you won't make me go home.

MARILYN: But you went anyway, not that day but the
day after. You went and waited with your family at
the kitchen table. David did not come home. I had the
Tempest towed into the shop. David did not come
home. I stood and stared at the empty box that had
held the transmission. Jean sat in the funeral home and
waited with her family. I authorized the purchase of
a rebuilt transmission. Jean waited for David to sit up
in his coffin and yell "Surprise!" He didn't. I drove the
Tempest home, parked it in the drive. They lowered
the coffin into the ground, and the earth began to pile
up on top of it and it was David's last chance to pull
the joke off, his last chance to leap out of the coffin
and laugh his loud laugh at his very good joke, his
best joke ever, he had taken them all in, it was a very
good joke but it was time for the joke to end. It was
time for David to pop up the lid like a Jack in the Box
and...but the weight of the earth would be too much
for him. All right—then he would dart from behind a
tombstone. Any minute now. He would flag down the
funeral procession on its way out of the cemetery. He
would beat them home and be waiting at the kitchen
table—having a late breakfast or lurking in the hallway
to chase Jean up the stairs—or lying on his bed in his
room reading science fiction—or barricaded in the
bathroom reading something else. He was in the living
room scuffing up the furniture with his big, boat sized
boots, and he was in the basement sneaking a smoke,
and he was out in the carport riding his first bicycle
and he was in the back yard mowing the lawn, and
he was everywhere in the house, in the yard, he was a
little boy and a grown, magnificent dark haired man.
So the day ended, and Jean and her family sat at the
kitchen table and they didn't wait any longer. David
was not coming home and they had to go on and they
would go on.

And as they sat there together the next morning at
breakfast, Jean's father believed for the first time that
they actually would. He was still drowning, he knew
they were all still drowning, but now and then as they
struggled up toward the surface, a luminous gray
patch of light appeared.

And then the letters David mailed on the day of his
death arrived like a giant meteor shower crashing
into earth, exploding entire continents, ripping the
atmosphere away.

So Jean returned to me, and the Tempest. She came up
for air—or tried to—in bed beside me. That was the
way I wanted it. We were young, and I loved her, and
I wanted to hold her and make it all right. I thought
that would be enough for her. I thought you could love
another person enough to be the thing that lets them
enter the world, and stand in it. But the world is full of
things that are falling.

I tried talking about it. *(To* JEAN*)* Jean—

JEAN: It's not that I don't want to talk about it, Marilyn.
I just don't know what to say.

MARILYN: *(To the audience)* I tried not talking about it.
*(To* JEAN*)* You hungry?

JEAN: I can't find anything to eat.

MARILYN: The refrigerator's filled with food.

JEAN: I'm sure that's true.

MARILYN: *(To the audience)* I tried— *(To* JEAN*)* Let's go
out.

JEAN: Where?

MARILYN: Where do you think?

JEAN: No.

MARILYN: Come on, Jean. You can say no to me—you
can say no to life—but you can't say no to— *(Singing)*

You deserve a break today...

JEAN: *(Laughing)* You're not fighting fair. That's a registered trademark. You're not authorized to use it redhead to redhead like that.

MARILYN: Come on, an official McDonaldland break is just what we need. We'll go out, we'll come back, and—

JEAN: Not yet, Marilyn.

MARILYN: But—

JEAN: I'm really not all that hungry, and I just don't want to, okay?

MARILYN: *(To the audience)* So I didn't push her, not right away. We had all the time in the world, didn't we? We were young, and I loved her, and we both had red hair. How could anything take that away?

*(The* TECHNICIANS *hand* MARILYN *two bottles of Fuchsia Plum. She hides them behind her back.)*

MARILYN: Guess what I've got...

JEAN: *(Not playing along)* Don't tell me...two packs of Camel Filters.

*(*MARILYN *produces the two bottles.)*

JEAN: You didn't!

MARILYN: I did!

JEAN: Fuchsia Plum! That is not a color found in nature, Marilyn.

MARILYN: Since when did the redheads let a thing like nature get in their way? *(Reading from the label)* Fuchsia Plum: A vibrant jewel tone for the modern woman who dares to say "I'm special."

JEAN: Fuchsia Plum is purple. Women who dye their hair purple are not saying they're special. They're screaming "I'm crazy" at the top of their lungs.

MARILYN: But Jean, it was your idea—

JEAN: I really should have dyed my hair black for the funeral. My roots were already coming in brown. Everyday, mousey, marrying brown. So. Take these back and get us two bottles of Midnight Minx. That is the appropriate color now.

MARILYN: *(Reaches out to touch and comfort* JEAN*)* Oh, Jean—

JEAN: *(Pulling away, as if* MARILYN'*s touch burns)* Don't touch me—

MARILYN: Jean!

JEAN: *(Horrified that she's said it out loud.)* I'm so sorry— oh, Marilyn, I didn't mean it. It's just it gets so close when you...I'm sorry.

MARILYN: *(Her back to* JEAN*)* It's all right.

JEAN: *(Pause. Desperate to apologize)* Maybe...maybe we should get out—go someplace—to dinner—

MARILYN: It'd be good for you, I know it would—

JEAN: Not for long, but—

MARILYN: We'll go to McDonald's—

JEAN: I don't know if McDonald's is such a good idea—

MARILYN: All right, we'll go someplace else—

JEAN: But I don't want to go someplace else. I want to go to McDonald's, only—

MARILYN: Only what?

JEAN: What if I start crying at McDonald's?

MARILYN: McDonald's is off limits for crying.

JEAN: But what if I do?

MARILYN: We are going to McDonald's. We are going to eat identical foods identically, ritualistically. Two French fries, one sip of coke, a bite of quarter pounder...with cheese. We are going to another McDonald's tomorrow night, and do it again. We are going to build you up one McDonald's at a time if it takes all year.

*(The* TECHNICIANS *create a welcoming doorway for McDonald's, each holding a tray with a Quarter Pounder with Cheese Meal, one for* MARILYN, *one for* JEAN. *The redheads almost make it to the doorway. But* JEAN *turns back.)*

JEAN: I can't.

MARILYN: Jesus Christ, Jean, you love McDonald's.

JEAN: Yes, I love McDonald's. And for a long, long time, I thought McDonald's loved me. But that's crazy. McDonald's is a multi-million dollar operation.

MARILYN: I don't want to talk about McDonald's anymore.

JEAN: You used to love it when I told the McDonald's story, remember?

MARILYN: That was when it was going to have a different ending.

JEAN: I can't help that.

MARILYN: Now all the McDonald's story means is that when you move to sit beside the Redhead on her bed, the phone will ring, and the story won't go on.

JEAN: I can't help that.

MARILYN: *(Exploding)* You could! If you loved me, you could help it! If you loved me—
I'm sorry. I know it's not your fault. I just don't know what to do.

JEAN: No. *I'm* sorry.

MARILYN: Don't be sorry. Be the redhead.

JEAN: I can't change it back. I was on my way to the Redhead's. The mythical, magical Redhead's. If I could just make it to the Redhead's... Well, I made it to the Redhead's. And the whole world changed. *(She turns to go.)* This is not—working, is it. I'd better go.

MARILYN: No, Jean, don't, if you leave now—

JEAN: I'll come back, and when I do, I'll be the redhead again.

MARILYN: You promise?

JEAN: Yes.

MARILYN: Cross your redhaired heart?

JEAN: Cross my redhaired heart.

MARILYN: All right. I'll wait. However long it takes. I'll wait. Cross my redhaired heart.

JEAN: I'll be the redhead. Next time.

MARILYN: *(The* TECHNICIANS *enter. One slips* MARILYN *into her robe. The other brings Jean the empty container of French fries. The* TECHNICIANS *leave.)* And two years later, here we stand.

JEAN: *(Turning back to* MARILYN*)* I did love you. I do love you.

MARILYN: If you love me, come to bed—

JEAN: No.

MARILYN: Let's get it over with, get it behind us, move on.

JEAN: As long as I stay here I'm safe.

MARILYN: From what?

JEAN: David's death.

MARILYN: That's not fair.

JEAN: Of course it's not fair. I love you.

MARILYN: If you love me—

JEAN: NO! As long as I stay here, the story about David is not about you.

MARILYN: That's your choice.

JEAN: It happened the way it happened. It tracked me down and it found me here. How can you say it was my choice? How can you say I had any choice in what happened here?

MARILYN: All right. But we can change it back.

JEAN: I can't. I'm sorry.

MARILYN: Don't be sorry, be the redhead.

JEAN: I can't.

MARILYN: Your choice.

JEAN: No.

MARILYN: It is.

JEAN: He did not choose to fall.

MARILYN: I don't care anymore, Jean—if he did, if he didn't. It's too long ago. We didn't know then, did we? We don't know now. We will never know. Are you telling me that knowing will change things for us?

JEAN: I can't change it back.

MARILYN: And I can't tell you why. That's what you really want from me, isn't it? You want me to make it all right. But I don't know why, and I can't make it all right. There are three things you can get if you come to bed with me. But one of them is never knowing why. You can't get that from me no matter how hard you try. And you have tried.
I don't care anymore Jean, I don't care. It's too long ago. We will never know.
Come to bed.

JEAN: Come to bed, come to bed, what did we do when I did come to bed? One kiss, two? We hated kissing each other.

MARILYN: We didn't.

JEAN: Liar.

MARILYN: Is that really the way you want the story to end, Jean? It is late when you arrive, you are tired, you come to bed, the phone rings, and we hated kissing each other?

*(No response from* JEAN*)*

MARILYN: All right, then. We hated kissing each other.

JEAN: We were going to be the aunts of each other's children. We were going to walk down the street together, pushing our baby carriages filled with redhair.

MARILYN: Wheel them down the street in matching prams.

JEAN: We could get by with words like pram when we were the redheads.

MARILYN: Oh. So you're saying we're not the redheads, is that what you came back to say?

JEAN: No—no—you know that's not—you know that's not what I want.

MARILYN: Then if you want something else—

JEAN: Not—not yet, Marilyn.

MARILYN: We agreed, Jean! This is our last chance redhaired plan. Now or never.

JEAN: Easy for you to say.

MARILYN: Easy?! *(She turns away from* JEAN.*)* I can't be the redhead alone anymore, Jean. I can't. So if you won't even try—

JEAN: What do you think all of this is! What else is it but trying!

MARILYN: I don't know. I know you think that if we start where we were, we can remember where we were going—but for some reason it doesn't ever work like that. We always just get stuck in before. And then you run away before we get to after.

JEAN: *(She takes a deep breath, tries to smile.)* I was really looking forward to coming here, to seeing you again. I'm sorry about all this other crap I can't help laying on you. *(She starts picking up all the French fries.)* I always think it will be different. I always think, we'll go back to where we were and start again, and it will have a different ending. I always think—I'm sorry, Marilyn. About everything. About that awful negligee. About these French fries. *(She takes a French fry off the bed, starts to eat it. Can't. She throws the rest of the French fries out.)* I shouldn't have gotten them. I haven't been able to eat a McDonald's French fry since…well, for a long time. I just can't seem to get it through my head. McDonald's *does not love me.* Anymore.
I'm sorry.

MARILYN: That's not what I want from you.

JEAN: What do you want?

MARILYN: Come to bed.

JEAN: *(She perches on the edge of the bed, awkwardly.)* Now what?

MARILYN: Comfortable?

JEAN: *(She moves so she is beside MARILYN.)* Yes.

MARILYN: Now you finish the McDonald's story. You finish the story that includes each of the billions sold. And then we go on. Wherever it is we're going. No matter what is left for us, together, after the story is finished. We go.

JEAN: I was at McDonald's, ordering a quarter pounder with cheese—

(JEAN *and* MARILYN *kiss.)*

JEAN: —a large coke—

(JEAN *and* MARILYN *kiss.)*

JEAN: —and a large fry.

(JEAN *and* MARILYN *kiss. From far away, the phone rings.)*

JEAN: And in a midtown Holiday Inn Hotel, my brother David wedged a chair against the door and lay down on a bed with a cigarette that did not know when to stop in one hand, and in the other the largest quantity of cocaine that the credit limit on his master charge could stand. He planned to slip quietly away from this world, on a bright, chemical dream. And instead, he woke up and found he had ridden into a trap. Oh, he had left this world, all right. No mistaking that. This world is easy to leave. Not the world he found himself in now. He found himself in a world that did not offer easy escape.
David woke up in hell, in a Holiday Inn Hotel room filled with flames. From the hallway, from the world he had left and to which he could not return, he heard the frenzied pounding on the door. He stood up, unsteady, confused. The things that were lacing up his life in the still, small places in his blood gave him no shade, no cool sweet resting place to hide from the crushing flames.
And the sounds of the sirens came to him. Called him to the window, where a fireman reached out his hand. But it was too late. The letters had been written, and sent and he was gone already, and so he went. The fire reached out to touch him as he started on his way down. He was my redhaired brother for the fourteen stories it took him to reach the ground.

My brother David was falling, a red halo around his head, and I was at McDonald's, and I was in your arms, and my brother David is falling, and I was ordering a quarter pounder with cheese, and I am in your arms, where my brother David is always falling. He will always be here falling, Marilyn. He will always be here. In this bed.

(MARILYN *gets out of bed, moves away from* JEAN.)

JEAN: I'm sorry, Marilyn. I'm—

MARILYN: *(Bitterly)* Yes. It is late when you arrive, and you are sorry. *(She lights a cigarette, does not offer one to Jean. Smokes alone.)* I wanted to be your redhaired twin, Jean. I really did.

JEAN: I know.

MARILYN: I tried.

JEAN: Sometimes I wish you hadn't tried so hard.

MARILYN: I'm still trying.

JEAN: But you'd like to stop.

MARILYN: I have to stop, Jean.

JEAN: Then stop, once and for all. Just stop and let this thing pass on by.

MARILYN: We'll have to start over, from scratch, we'll have to start over and we can't ever be the redheads again.

*(One of the stage* TECHNICIANS *enters, and removes or changes one aspect of the redhead world.)*

JEAN: Not even at Christmas?

MARILYN: Not even at Christmas.

*(The other stage* TECHNICIAN *enters, and the redhead world is swiftly dismantled.)*

JEAN: And at our weddings, we can't be bridesmaids?

MARILYN: No, we'll send each other invitations, along with a hundred others. We'll send a gift but we won't come.

JEAN: I read this story, a long time ago, about two girls playing on a school playground, each wearing the exact same plaid dress. One was on the teeter-totter. A hideous freak wind came along and swept her away, they never saw her again. Well, the other girl wearing the same dress saw it all and went insane.

MARILYN: I was watching an old episode of E R the other day. I only caught the tail end of it, but it was about a man who had a twin brother who was in for emergency surgery. Well, the brother insisted that everything his brother felt, he felt too. So they wheel the sick one into the operating room, and start to cut, and the other brother drops writhing to the floor. He describes the incision, he feels the knife probing inside him. "Get this man into surgery" the young but oddly competent doctor commands. "You're not going to operate!", the competent but oddly sexy nurse protests. "No", he replies, "But we're going to get him under anesthesia, do everything we can. I told him earlier we've never lost the brother of a patient yet." Poignant pause. "Now I'm not so sure."
I can't make it all right, Jean. I have to stop trying. I love you, but I have to stop.

*(The redhaired world has been erased, transformed back to the ordinary.)*

JEAN: *(Watching the* TECHNICIANS *carry off the last of the redhead world.)* We're not the redheads any longer?

MARILYN: No. Not ever again.

JEAN: It shouldn't have happened like this.

MARILYN: But it did.

JEAN: Maybe if we—

MARILYN: What?

JEAN: Maybe if we went to every McDonald's in America, a sort of pilgrimage—

MARILYN: We could go to every McDonald's in the world, and it wouldn't change what happens when we do this.

(MARILYN *kisses* JEAN, JEAN *pulls away.*)

MARILYN: Wake up, Jean, we're not the redheads any longer. The McDonald's story don't cut no shit with me.

JEAN: Then what does?

MARILYN: Good question.

JEAN: Marilyn—

MARILYN: Yes?

JEAN: Do you think that in a parallel redhaired world where the McDonald's story still cuts through—

MARILYN: Jean, don't—

JEAN: Last time, I promise.

MARILYN: Cross your redhaired heart?

JEAN: You're as bad as me.

MARILYN: You promise this is the last time?

JEAN: Yes.

MARILYN: Okay.

JEAN: Do you think that in the parallel redhaired world, where the McDonald's story still cuts through all the shit there is, that even though David is not alive, even though the phone call came, and all the things that came with it came on and on—do you think that the redheads are still the redheads? Do you think they still love each other?

MARILYN: Yes.

JEAN: Good.

MARILYN: Is that enough?

JEAN: *(She returns to the Tempest area. To the audience)*
I will never know if the deaths that were David's to
carry grew too heavy, and had to be set aside. It is
also possible that he tried to move too quickly toward
someone he loved—the monster that he carried on his
back shifted unexpectedly, catching David off balance,
he struggled for a moment, but then—then the weight
was gone. It must have seemed to him that angels felt
no lighter than he did, for that one, long instant before
he hit the ground.
And his fall, that was a leap, from a high place, landed
right on top of me. David's death piled up on top of
me. And kept me from taking a single step toward a
person I loved. *(She gets into the Tempest.)* I was driving
along, and I saw this woman, crossing the street to
the side of me. And I smiled, because it was you,
Marilyn. You the way you would look when you were
sixty-five. There—that's Marilyn at sixty-five, I said
to myself. And I smiled. You were someone's mother,
someone's grandmother, someone's aunt. You were
carrying a red bag, and your hair was gray, and you
were very nice and neat, you looked good. You looked
very good. I could see that you had lived through the
redhaired death nicely—I could see it from the way
you moved across the street. And I wanted to call out
to you and tell you that I had too. I wanted to tell you
that I had learned how to shoulder the weight—that I
had learned how to carry it.
And I wanted to tell you that I had learned that it is not
the weight of our deaths, in the end, that is the hardest
thing to carry. It is our regret. For all the steps we
wanted to take, and didn't, toward someone we love.
I wanted so badly to call out to you, to say "Marilyn,
I'm all right."

*(Lights fade on* MARILYN.*)*

JEAN: And that was the last time I saw you.

*(Blackout)*

## END OF PLAY